Why Do My Characters Behave That Way?

Three Aspects of Character Development

By Janie Sullivan

Other books by Janie Sullivan

Non-Fiction

Janie's Memoir Writing Class:

A Memoir Guide/Workbook for Those Who Have
Reached a "Certain Age"

Do You Call Yourself a Writer?

Develop and Deliver an Online Course

A Tuscan Dining Experience

Creating Characters That Speak:
Using Character Sketches and Dialogue Effectively

Writing from A to Z:
A Blog Series from The Center for Writing Excellence

Mini Lessons in Story Starting
Three Quick Lessons for Fiction Writers

Family Anthology:
How to Turn Your Family Files into a Book the Whole Family
Can Enjoy

A System of Five:
Five Practices that Guarantee Excellent Faculty

Anthologies

Picking Dandelions
The Johnston Family Anthology

First, Second, and Third Annual Fiction Anthologies
(Center for Writing Excellence Anthologies)

Fiction

The Wise Acres Cozy Mystery Series

Book One: *The Mahjong Murder Club*

Book Two: *Fortune or Folly??* (Due Spring, 2018)

Co-Authored Fiction
with Rhonda Jackson

Alexis' Aggravation:
Murder in the Southwest

One Hundred Years From London
Volume of Short Stories for Light Reading

All books can be found at Janie Sullivan's Author Page on
Amazon.com: http://www.amazon.com/-/e/B008S027GO

Why do my Characters Behave that Way?

Three Aspects of Character Development

Why do my Characters Behave That Way?

All rights reserved.

Copyright © 2018 by Janie Sullivan

All rights reserved. No part of this book may be used or reproduced by any means, graphic, electronic, or mechanical, including photocopying, recording, taping or by any information storage retrieval system without the written permission of the publisher except in the case of brief quotations embodied in critical articles and reviews. This is a work of fiction. All of the characters, names, incidents, organizations, and dialogue in this novel are either the products of the authors' imaginations or are used fictitiously.

For information:

The Center for Writing Excellence, a Small Press
480 Bray Central Drive, #11204
Allen, Texas 75013

Janie's Email: janiewrites1@gmail.com

ISBN-13: 978-1985305700

ISBN-10: 1985305704

Published by: The Center for Writing Excellence, a Small Press
Printed in the United States of America
Date: February, 2018

Table of Contents

Why do My Characters Behave That Way?

In this booklet, you will learn about how your characters got the way they are. You will also learn about how to handle a motivationally complicated character and how to create a humorous character. When you finish, you should be able to, if not completely control your characters, at least understand a bit more about why they do what they do.

What is the Character Really Like?

We all wear masks at one time or another. Think about the last time you were in a room full of people and wished you were somewhere else. What did your 'mask' tell the people around you? Did the person you were smiling at really know you were actually bored, angry, sad, or exhausted? Maybe, but more likely not.

Your characters wear masks, too. Sometimes the character has trouble expressing emotion. For example, an elderly man who was never demonstrative has a hard time saying, "I love you" to a grandchild and the grandchild feels unloved. Or a teenage girl who everyone thinks is a "good girl" is disturbed by the overtly sexual feelings she has toward another character in the story. She hides behind her "good girl" mask while secretly yearning for some very illicit erotic contact.

Sometimes the character will drop the mask and show her true self, much to the surprise of the rest of the characters. This can be used as a tool for twisting the plot – nobody expected him to be the culprit! Showing your characters' true self will make them seem more real to the reader, creating a connection that will help the story move along.

There is also the danger of confusing the reader if the true self of the character is shown in a way that is not realistic or doesn't make sense. The key to success in fiction lies with the characters and the connection between them and the reader. An excellent way to have conflict in a story is to have the character's outer mask and inner true self conflict in such a way that the reader connects with the character and wants to keep reading to see how that conflict is resolved.

Backstory: How the Character Got to be Like That

The protagonist, or main character, just like you and me, is the product of his or her backstory. Characters do not just appear fully formed and ready to be inserted into the story. However, if you have a 30-year old main character it would be not only be impractical, but also impossible to tell the entire back-story when introducing the character.

You, the writer, will choose the parts that you believe the reader needs to know in order to understand the character. The key is being able to determine just what those parts are and how to include them. Much of this will depend on the kind of story, and the role of the character in the story.

There may be no information at all about some characters in short stories until the character appears and does or says something. It is not important for the reader to know how the character will respond until he or she responds, but it is critical for the writer to know WHY the character responds the way he or she does to a certain situation.

Example: In the second paragraph of a fiction story written by Janie Sullivan and Rhonda Jackson, we find these comments:

Now the cops are here. You know, I gave up all that cop stuff. I got tired of all the dead bodies they found when I worked nights in homicide. Owning a quiet little pub across the street from the Convention and Opera House sounded so nice. I even got an antique oak bar from an old speak-easy in Chicago. And now, dead bodies are landing in my lap again. This is so aggravating. (Sullivan & Jackson, Alexis Aggravation, Murder in the Southwest, 2015)

We know that these are the thoughts of the protagonist because they are in first person. They are not spoken aloud to anyone, but they give us a bit of the backstory. In one short paragraph we learn that the character used to be a police officer, but has left that job (we don't know why, other than he or she was burned out – is there something else that precipitated the leaving?) and now owns a small bar in the downtown area (assumed because of the location of the pub across from the

Convention and Opera House). We also discover that the main character is not happy about being dragged back into a police situation.

Based on this paragraph alone, what is the picture you have of the protagonist? Do you identify with him or her? Is the character believable? Do you know anything about the motivation of the character? What other information do you want about the character?

Motivation: You want WHAT?

Your reader will simply not believe the concept or premise of the story if there is no motivation. The characters will have a reason (or reasons) for doing what they do. In the story above, we can surmise that the character is not happy about being dragged back into a police situation. In fact, we don't actually know if that will happen, but if it does, what would be the motivation?

The conflict might be that he or she is not happy, but for some reason is going to be involved. As we read further we will want to discover that motivation – or else we won't believe the story and will lose our connection. Here is an example from further along in the story that gives us a clue about how the main character feels about police work:

The old man's information did make me wonder about things. "Oh no, Alexis!" I told myself. "You are NOT a cop anymore!" (Sullivan & Jackson, Alexis Aggravation, Murder in the Southwest, 2015)

To discover the motivation, it is helpful to go back to your character list and think about each character. What is the conflict the character will be facing? What will motivate him or her to overcome that conflict?

Consider the villain in the story the same way. Why did he or she do the villainous act? If the writer knows the answer to that question, he or she can then get the character to act in certain ways that will give clues to the reader without giving away the ending.

The backstory, which leads to the motivation, is not always readily apparent in the story, but the writer needs to know what it is in order to create the tension and suspense in the story. The conflict needs to be realistic, so the reader understands what the character is going through, but it does not need to be spelled out. Let the reader make assumptions and connections with the point of view characters on his or her own. And, keep the element of surprise to yourself until you are ready to expose it.

Of Course the Character Wants That!

Think about your character before you determine how much backstory to put in. For example, if your main character is a super hero, the reader already knows much about the motivation. Super heroes are the good guys, they are always fighting evil to make the world a better place for those who don't have super powers. Writers don't need a lot of backstory or motivation explanation with super heroes.

Another obvious example where the reader already knows what the character wants is if the protagonist is a selfish, greedy, sleazy lawyer. The reader is not surprised to discover that the character is out to swindle anyone he or she can to get ahead.

Also, if the main character is a woman whose goal is to go to medical school and the story is set in 2017, there are no surprises there. It is not at unusual at all for a woman to aspire to medical school today and no reason to include a lot of backstory or motivation; but if the story is set in 1913, the desire for a woman to become a doctor is completely out of character. In the latter case, the writer would have to include some backstory and motivation indicators to let the reader know WHY the character wants to become a doctor.

There are ways to insert backstory and motivation into the story without boring the reader with paragraphs of narrative. The key is to present the right amount of information at the right time without interrupting the story in a way that will confuse the reader or make him or her impatient with the flow of the story.

Hints and Brief Details

Dropping a hint here and there is probably the easiest way to insert backstory or motivation. Just make sure the hints do not give away the plot, but do make the reader think, "While I did not expect that person to be the villain, when I look back at the story, it makes sense." Here is an example from the story we have been looking at:

…another detective, his perfectly tailored Armani suit looking completely out of place… (Sullivan & Jackson, Alexis Aggravation, Murder in the Southwest, 2015)

It's just a hint, doesn't really tell us anything right now, other than this particular detective has expensive taste in clothes. Later on in the story, that detail will make sense.

Some other things that can be used to provide hints without giving away the plot are:

- A casual reference to a phone call made earlier to a relative or friend in an unusual situation (prison, away at camp, etc.)
- A framed university diploma on the wall.
- A worn toy reverently placed on a mantle in a childless couple's home.
- A description of something that is now very different from what it once was. *Example: There was a time, before the war, when the sagging, rusty front gate swung proudly on sturdy, oiled hinges.*

When using this technique, don't provide so much detail that the reader will immediately figure out the end of the story. You want to put enough in just enough detail that the reader doesn't look at it as a "clue" at the time he or she reads it, but enough to make the reader nod his or her head and think about it when the villain is revealed.

Inserted Paragraph

Another tactic is to insert a paragraph or two explaining something or giving the reader a quick glimpse of the past. While this does interrupt the story, if it is short it will not jar the reader out of the story. You will want to segue into the backstory paragraph, giving the reader a hint about what you are about to do. A good way to do this is to insert a transition statement at the end of a paragraph or the beginning of the next paragraph that will lead the reader into the inserted information.

In this example from another of Janie Sullivan's fiction stories, *The Duplicate Saloon*, three old friends run into each other after several years of separation. The transition statement is the first one in the paragraph after they discover each other:

It took a few minutes for everyone to recover their surprise at seeing each other again. The last time these three were together was on a riverboat out of St. Louis. Angie was one of the hostesses and Doc and Snake Eye were playing poker. Angie, who was young, slender and pretty, enraptured both the gun fighters. The three of them had a high old time on that riverboat trip. When the trip was over, Angie declared she did not want to give up her life as a riverboat princess to go live in the Wild West with either of the gun slinging gamblers, although they both asked.

In the years since that river trip, the gun fighters went their separate ways out West. Doc hired himself out as a part time lawman to small towns in Montana and Wyoming Territories. Snake Eye continued to gamble his way through Colorado, Utah and now in to Arizona Territory, staying just barely on the wrong side of the law. Angie's fortunes steadily decreased until she found herself working in this tiny, desolate bar in Dry Gulch, Arizona. (Sullivan, The Duplicate Saloon: One Hundred Years from London, 2016, p. 41)

While these two paragraphs momentarily take the reader out of the story, they do not interrupt the flow and add valuable information about the relationship between the three characters. We are also given the opportunity to gain the following information:

- **Knowledge of previous events**. We learned that the three met at an earlier time on a river boat gambling adventure. They were all more prosperous at that time and both cowboys desired the affections of the woman.
- **Foreshadowing**. Something is probably going to happen in the future regarding this past relationship.
- **Characterization**. We know that the woman liked the life of a riverboat princess but was not able to maintain

it. We also discover that the two cowboys parted ways –
one on each side of the law.

- **Reader interest**. What questions do these two passages
  raise in your mind? How does this information add to
  your interest in the story of these three characters?

Flashback

Flashbacks are more detailed insertions in the story. They often
contain full dialogue, description, action, etc. Flashbacks are
NOT part of the story time – they describe actions that occurred
before the current story is taking place. Follow these guidelines
when including flashbacks in your story:

1. Include enough interesting information before the
   flashback so the reader is already committed to the story.
   Flashing back too soon will confuse the reader. The
   reader should know enough about the characters and
   the current situation that the flashback will not confuse
   him or her.
2. Never use the flashback as the beginning of the story.
   Ask yourself these questions:
   a. Who are the characters?
   b. What is their current relationship?
   c. Where are they now?
   d. Why should the reader care?
3. The flashback can be the second scene in the story if the
   first scene is compelling enough to make the reader care
   about what happened in the past.

4. Don't put everything in the flashback. Let the reader draw his or her own conclusions with a bit of information, don't tell the reader every little thing about what happened in the past.

5. Consider starting the story earlier in time if you find you need to flashback frequently to clarify events in the current story line.

Exposition

Exposition is simply stopping the story dead and including the backstory. This can be dangerous so only do it if you really need to. You may lose your reader entirely if you are not careful when stopping a story dead in its tracks. Two reasons you may need to do this are:

1. Some characters' histories are so detailed the only way they can be included is through unbroken narrative and description. Do this only if detailed knowledge of the history is crucial to the story line.

2. Sometimes the back story is so interesting that the reader won't get restless wanting to get back to the current story. If the reader is fascinated by this interesting history and it adds understanding to the current story, then include it.

Straightforward Emotion

This is the formula for emotion in a fiction story: Desire Creates Emotion.

Your character may be either acting in accord with his/her desires and emotions or there may be conflict here. Writing emotion into your story is done essentially the same way in either case, but if there is conflict, there are other aspects to consider when writing emotion. In this section, we will talk about inserting straightforward emotion into the story.

Including emotion is one of those "show, don't tell" events in a fiction story. If you are trying to convey the fact that someone is afraid, you could say, *Ric was afraid of them and what they might do.* However, it would be much more effective to show the reader how Ric was reacting to them: *"No. No!" Ric tugged at his seatbelt, his sweaty hands slipping on the buckle. "You can't take my soul! You can't."* (Jackson, 2016, p. 119)

Here the author is using actions, dialogue and bodily sensation to convey the idea that the character, Ric, is very afraid.

Actions

In the example the words *...tugged at his seatbelt...* are action words describing what Ric was doing. They convey a sense of urgency (*his sweaty hands slipping on the buckle*) and tell the reader that Ric is trapped by the belt.

Dialogue

The dialogue used obviously tells the reader that Ric doesn't want something to happen – and at the end of the passage the reader finds out what he is afraid of.

Bodily Sensations

The bodily sensations that the reader notices are the feeling of the seatbelt not opening, the feeling of being trapped, and a level of panic that suggests that Ric may be sweating in fear.

Deceptive Emotion

This is emotion that is in conflict with the behavior that is being exhibited. This happens when a character wants to hide how he or she really feels about something. You can show this in a number of ways, and sometimes a subtle reference to something may work better than saying it bluntly like this:

She screamed at the boys advancing on her little sister, begging them not to hurt her, but inside she was thrilled at the prospect of seeing her sister suffer.

A better way to show the conflict is through action, dialogue, and possibly thoughts. In this example, we see that Julie is really not interested in saving her sister but is actually happy as the prospect that she might be getting hurt. She does make an effort at the beginning to stop them but is not very serious about it.

Julie stepped in front of the advancing boys, an odd, almost thrilling, light in her eyes for a moment, then half-heartedly tried to stop them, stepping aside at the last minute to reveal her little sister quaking in terror behind her.

The Motivationally Complicated Character

In fiction, just as in real life, characters can want more than one thing, feel more than one emotion, and even change their minds about how they feel or what they want. People are not one-dimensional, and neither should your characters be. Complex characters feel more real to readers, if they are not so complex that the reader becomes very confused. The complexity you build into your characters should also be believable and relevant to the story. It is certainly plausible to have the quiet, unassuming librarian in a murder mystery live a double life as a serial killer, but would you add that element into a romance?

Values, Desires, and Inner Turmoil

The collision of values in real life makes things interesting. When you value being slim and trim and someone presents you with an ice cream sundae complete with caramel sauce, nuts, and whipped cream, your value of tasting sweet things meets head on with the desire to stay slim and trim. What happens? Do you accept the ice cream? Or do you forego it for another day?

Your characters will also face decisions like this throughout the story when their values collide. This is a good way to build tension in a story. Let your reader see the dilemma the character is going through every time a decision comes up that could potentially change the direction of the story.

Conflicting values are at the heart of any ethical conflict, whether internal or external. In fiction writing, the internal conflicts and their resolution become excellent vehicles for providing backstory for characters. There are times when two values will collide, and one will win out. In other circumstances, the values may collide, and the other value will win. For example, in this country we are fortunate to be able to practice free speech, under Article 19 of the Declaration Human Rights. Public safety is also an expectation protected by law.

Courts have ruled that the right to free speech trumps the right to public safety related to tracking down criminals, therefore journalists do not have to reveal their sources, even if they are criminals. On the other hand, the right to public safety out ranks freedom of speech if you are tempted to shout FIRE! in a crowded theater.

You can create characters with more than one desire, making them believable and greatly enhancing your fiction.

Giving Your Characters Two Desires

You can use a scene to showcase the two desires or values your character has in a way that does not have to advance the plot, but instead gives some useful information about the character. For example, create a scene where the main character, who has a secret crush on a married character, writes a love letter to the character, and fanaticizes about how the character will respond, like having them run off into the sunset together. Now have the first character tear up the love letter and flush it down the toilet. This scene does nothing for the plot because nothing happens because of the letter, but it can be used to foreshadow a much larger event to come later. It also gives the reader some information about the character. The reader now knows that the character may not act upon his or her desires, but instead fanaticizes about them, then discards them.

In the end of the story, the character may exhibit a different outcome when it comes to acting upon those desires, showing growth in the character. Using small conflicts to build the character and give the reader a complete picture of how the character responds to his or her conflicting values will make the character more realistic and believable for the reader.

What are some conflicting values you can incorporate into your characters that will provide insight to their personalities and remain relevant to the story?

Using Dialogue to Dramatize Value

Dialogue is an effective way to show the reader what values cause the character to struggle. You can use internal dialogue, dialogue between the character and someone else, or by eavesdropping on a conversation where others are talking about the character. Here are some examples:

Internal Dialogue

She sighed, lips flapping over empty gums while her teeth rested in a glass of murky water on the bedside table. Her surprisingly bright blues eyes closed and she thought, "I'm afraid to sleep, afraid not to sleep." (Sullivan, Visiting Granny: One Hundred Years from London, 2016, p. 86)

Dialogue Between the Character and Someone Else

"Here it is, and just in time, too." Luanda shook the tiny jar, rattling the contents to get Eloise's attention.

"Humph! I don't know how you do it, but you always do come through in the end." Eloise smiled indulgently and took the jar from Luanda, opened it and carefully sprinkled the contents into the pot. There was a faint hissing sound as she slid the spoon back into the pot and started stirring again. "Thanks, honey. I am sorry I yelled at you. It is just that this is so important right now and you do tend to get distracted very easily, especially this time of the year." (Sullivan, Trial Run: One Hundred Years from London, 2016)

Dialogue Between Other Characters

"You're sure? It was JW?" Abigail remembered the odd conversation she'd had with JW the previous morning. "Poor Lucy! She must be devastated!" Although supposedly a secret, the engagement of JW Booth and Lucy Hale was known throughout the theater community. It was a recent development but had not been formally announced.

"I'm sure she wasn't aware of JW's feelings about the President."
Joseph played the role of Asa in the play. He'd worked with Booth in
the past and was well aware of the rancor JW held for the President.
Joseph and Abigail were standing beyond the lines of soldiers blocking
the theater, away from the crowds circling around, quietly discussing
the assassination.

"It's lucky the engagement hadn't been announced, so she should be
spared any embarrassment or ill treatment." (Jackson, Finding
Booth: One Hundred Years from London, 2016)

You can use narrative to explain to the reader that the character
is suffering conflicting values, but it is more effective to show
the reader through conversation. The dialogue will draw the
reader into the scene rather than just let the reader observe
what is going on.

The Dual Emotion

Cultural preferences and previous experiences can also affect a
character's emotional response to a situation, sometimes
ending up with contradictory emotions. Think about the
emotional responses you have to the people you interact with
daily. You may like someone as a person, but possibly fear that
same person as a boss. On the other hand, you may be repulsed
by someone who has multiple tattoos but are secretly attracted
to that same person because he or she exhibits an aura of danger
or forbiddingness; a trait you wish you possessed.

Your characters can also have dual, often conflicting, emotional responses to situations or other characters. The first thing you must do is make the reader understand the reasons behind the contradictory emotions.

For example, if your heroine is attracted to the very manly, virile lead male character, but scared to death of men because of a terrible incident when she was in her early teens, you need to, without "telling" show that, although she wants the man, she knows she can never get close to him. This is the prevailing theme of romance novels, but it can also be applied in other fiction.

In Summary

When a character has mixed feelings toward another character, you can take some steps:

- Identify in your own mind what emotions the character is feeling.
- Check to see if you have done the groundwork for these mixed feelings by dramatizing the causes of each. If not, you may need to go back and add one or more earlier scenes.
- Decide if you want to portray the contradictory feelings in alternate scenes, in the same scene, through exposition, or in some combination of these.

- Include sufficient emotional indicators for the reader to experience each emotion.

Complicated characters often hold two conflicting values and/or desires. Whichever path the character chooses gives the reader some valuable insight to that character's personality and beliefs. Consider all the choices the character makes in the story: the small choices should coincide with and sometimes even foreshadow the larger choices made later in the story.

Emotional Mini-Bio

Use the following questions to discover the emotional values of each of your characters:

1. What is the character's name?
2. What three or four things does this person value most in life? (i.e., success, money, family, God, love, integrity, power, peace and quiet, etc.)
3. What three or four things does this person most fear?
4. What is this person's basic underlying attitude about life? (i.e., "Things will turn out all right." Or "They're all out for themselves." Or "It's best to expect nothing so you won't be disappointed.")
5. What does he or she need to know about a person to accept him or her as trustworthy?
6. What would cause this person more pain than anything else?
7. What would this person consider the most wonderful thing that could ever happen to him or her?
8. What three words would this person use to describe him or herself? (Accurate or not)
9. How accurate is the self-description?
10. What organization embodies this person's values? (i.e., Mensa, Daughters of the American Revolution, church, Aryan Pride, PTA)
11. Does he or she belong to the organization? Why or why not?

The Humorous Character

When thinking about writing humor into your story, it is important to remember that not everyone has the same sense of humor so what one person thinks is funny, another might not be amused at all. Don't let this discourage you. Write what you think is funny and those readers who have a similar sense of humor as you will appreciate the humor.

Humor can range from gentle to much more raucous. Sometimes people will exhibit what is commonly called a 'dry' sense of humor. My dad was like that. Most of the time he was quiet and reserved. He had a very strong moral sense and generally did not appreciate off-color jokes or somewhat 'shady' humor. Every once in a while, though, he would say something that would cause anyone near to turn their heads in astonishment, wondering if he actually said whatever it was that was funny. He would return our stares with his usual serious countenance, but we could see laughter in the squint of his eyes or the slightly upturned corners of his mouth. It made him more real to the rest of us.

Types of Humor

No matter what the level of humor is, the basic techniques for writing it remain the same. There are three techniques: exaggeration, ridicule, and reversal of expectations. You can use any combination of one, two or all three techniques to create your funny character.

Exaggeration

Exaggeration in a comic character means the reader is not supposed to believe the character really exists. The character is not just larger than life, the character is simply unbelievable. Take a normal, but somewhat eccentric behavior of someone and expand upon it. An easy one is to use the butler. For some reason, butlers are funny just being butlers, but you can exaggerate on some attributes of the butler even more to make a character that is not completely believable, but one that can be imagined. What are some attributes of butlers that you can elaborate on to make the character a funny one?

Another thing you can do to create your exaggerated character is to play one of those silly games you see on Facebook occasionally. The last one I saw was this:

Name the color of your pants and the last thing you ate. This is the name of your band. In my case, my band name was *Blue Cheerios*. What is your band name?

I have also seen alphabetized lists of attributes in one column and other alphabetized attributes in a second column. All of the attributes refer to something similar, like Arizona plants or desert heat references. Take the word that starts with the first letter of your first name from the first column and add the word from the second column that starts with the first letter of your last name to form a new name. You can come up with some funny names this way.

Exaggeration can also be subtle or applied to only the subsidiary characters. Keep your main characters true to their characterization but put an odd side character in there somewhere. Perhaps a town drunk provides some comic relief in otherwise tense situations. This is an effective way to dispel tension without pulling the main characters out of character.

For example, if you are writing a very tense scene where someone is about to do something he or she really does not want to do but doesn't know how to get out of the situation, you can have the comic relief character burst in, stopping the action. Be sure to build up the tension so the reader is as relieved as the character is when the action is interrupted by the comic relief character.

You also need to think about the entire story, how plausible do you want it to be? If the entire story is meant to be a comedy, then use exaggeration throughout, but if it is an otherwise serious story, use exaggeration only to relieve tension or make transitions.

In this example, from the Alexis Murder Series by Janie Sullivan and Rhonda Jackson, a somewhat humorous character is introduced to explain a situation:

I took over the Red Herring when my parents were killed while on a cruise the year before. I was on medical leave from the police force because Lucky Louie shot me while I was trying to arrest him for exposing himself to a group of senior citizens getting off a bus. They were on a tour, hoping to see some 'authentic cowboys' in action. I don't think they were impressed with the show put on by Lucky Louie, one of our local characters. I don't think Louie meant to shoot me, either, but he got his gun caught in the holster when he pulled down his pants to moon the tour bus. He was drunk, too. Anyhow, the bullet in my left knee took me out of commission for a while. (Sullivan & Jackson, Alexis Aggravation, Murder in the Southwest, 2015)

Ridicule and Satire

Ridicule can be used when the writer likes the character but wants to portray him or her with characteristics that are silly, but not hurtful. Sort of the likeable buffoon, if you will. Using gentle ridicule to describe a character, usually a secondary one, is a effective way to get the reader to chuckle and to like the character, even though he or she might be a bit goofy.

Another method of injecting humor into a story is through satire. Satire can be used to portray someone who is laughable, but not dangerous. Carry the ridicule or satire too far, and the humor is lost because the character becomes scary. Some things to think about when using ridicule or satire include:

- Characters need to be representative of the institution or other segment of society you are satirizing. For example, if you want to ridicule a group of people who represent a segment of the rich and famous, then make sure you are clear in who your target is.
- Don't make generalizations but be specific. Here is an example: In the novel *Dodsworth*, by Sinclaire Lewis, one of the characters is based on his first wife. He exaggerates her self-centeredness, snobbishness, and habit of belittling others. The result of this exaggerated ridicule is a satirizing of a certain kind of upper-class female: expensive, spoiled, idle, and useless.

You can base your characters on someone you know and then exaggerate their normal characteristics to the point of ridicule, creating a humorous character who does things some of us would really WANT to do, but don't dare for fear of being laughed at.

Think of a person from your past that was not nice. Take one of the unsavory characteristics of that person and exaggerate on it, creating a character that has one very ridiculous characteristic. Make it a funny one.

Startled into Laughter

This occurs when the character does or says something completely unexpected. If a character who has been portrayed throughout the story as a very prim and proper person, with a high moral standard and one that is very aware of social comportment does something out of character, not only will the reader chuckle, but the character's reaction to the out of character behavior can be a source of humor as well.

For example, you can write a scene in a crime story where everyone is quite serious, discussing aspects of the crime, taking notes, interviewing bystanders, etc. when the lead detective, usually very serious and on track, suddenly burps very loud. Everyone around stops what they are doing, looks at the detective, tries not to laugh, and looks down at what they were doing when he glares around the room. The scene is tense right now – and the detective suddenly laughs aloud and says, *"Hey, lighten up! It was a great taco."*

Tone, the Big Picture

Ultimately, the overall tone of the story or book is going to determine the amount of humor you add to it or even if you add humor at all. Any scene can be written as humorous, witty, scary, sad, or ominous. You, as the author, decide which it will be, and then you convince your reader that you are right. To convince your reader that you think something is funny, you must believe it is funny.

You also need to look at the entire book or story: Does the humor fit? Is it appropriate? Is it placed correctly? Humor comes in many forms and can be subtle, obvious, or over the top. Humor cannot be explained. If you must tell the reader something is funny, it won't be funny. The tone of the book, article, and scene will let the reader know this is funny.

How characters react to a statement or situation will help determine the level of humor in the scene. Don't try to force the humor, or it will fall flat.

References

Jackson, R. (2016). *Finding Booth: One Hundred Years from London.* Apache Junction: Center for Writing Excellence.
Jackson, R. (2016). *The Gift: One Hundred Years from London.* Apache Junction: Center for Writing Excellence.
Sullivan, J. (2016). *The Duplicate Saloon: One Hundred Years from London.* Apache Junction: Center for Writing Excellence.
Sullivan, J. (2016). *Trial Run: One Hundred Years from London.* Apache Junction: Center for Writing Excellence.
Sullivan, J. (2016). *Visiting Granny: One Hundred Years from London.* Apache Junction: Center for Writing Excellence.
Sullivan, J., & Jackson, R. (2015). *Alexis Aggravation, Murder in the Southwest.* Apache Junctoin: Center for Writing Excellence.

About the Author

Janie Sullivan, MBA, MAEd, has been teaching adult learners for over 25 years. She has taught online over 20 years, specializing in writing, communications, and small business applications. She was a faculty trainer for over 15 years at both the University and Community College levels. She has been published in several newspapers, magazines and online sites. She has a strong entrepreneurial background, having run a very successful project management documentation production company during the 90s.

Education
Masters of Business Administration
Masters of Education Administration
Bachelor of Arts in Journalism

Publications and Courses Written
21-courses in a Certificate of Online Teaching Strategies
Novel: Alexis' Aggravation: Murder in the Southwest
Cozy Mystery Series: Wise Acres Cozy Mysteries, Book One: Mahjong Mystery Club. Book Two: Fortune or Folly?? (Due out in Spring 2018)
Anthology: One Hundred Years from London, Short Stories for Light Reading

Articles in Various Publishing Venues		
Newspapers	**Websites**	**Magazines**
The Missoulian	eHow	Small Business
The Phillipsburg	Infobarrel	Start-Up
Mail	Demand Studios	Magazine
The Mesa Tribune	Examiner.com	The Adjunct
The Business	Suite 101	Advocate
Journal	HubPages